How to Draw & Paint Tractors, Trucks and Trains

by

Helen Webster

ARCTURUS

Arcturus Publishing Ltd
26/27 Bickels Yard
151–153 Bermondsey Street
London SE1 3HA

Published in association with
foulsham
W. Foulsham & Co. Ltd,
The Publishing House, Bennetts Close, Cippenham,
Slough, Berkshire SL1 5AP, England

ISBN 0-572-03011-8

British Library Cataloguing-in-Publication Data: a catalogue record for this book is available from the British Library

Copyright © 2004 Arcturus Publishing Limited

All rights reserved

The Copyright Act prohibits (subject to certain very limited exceptions) the making of copies of any copyright work or of a substantial part of such a work, including the making of copies by photocopying or similar process. Written permission to make a copy or copies must therefore normally be obtained from the publisher in advance. It is advisable also to consult the publisher if in any doubt as to the legality of any copying which is to be undertaken.

Editor: Sarah Kovandzich
Text design: Chris Smith
Cover design: Emma Avery

Printed in Singapore

Dorset Libraries
Withdrawn Stock

contents

introduction

This fun and informative handbook is essential for any budding artist who loves to draw big moving vehicles and machinery.

The book begins by teaching you some basic techniques for drawing trucks, trains and tractors. Each of the drawing activities breaks down objects into simple shapes and patterns – to make sure you know exactly what to do in every step, you'll see that I've shaded the parts of the picture you need to work on next.

As you work through the book, you will learn new skills to make your pictures more detailed and you'll be able to experiment with using a wide range of materials.

Every chapter of the book forms a mini art class. Just follow the step-by-step instructions and by the end of the book, you will have quite a few secret art tricks up your sleeve!

You won't need lots of art materials for every activity – as long as you have a pencil and rubber, you're ready to get started. So, let's begin.

how to draw a truck using simple shapes

A truck is easy to draw using lines, rectangles, squares and circles.

In each of the steps below (and on the following pages) the part of the picture you need to draw is shaded with a colour – but don't colour in your own picture until you have finished drawing it.

you will need:

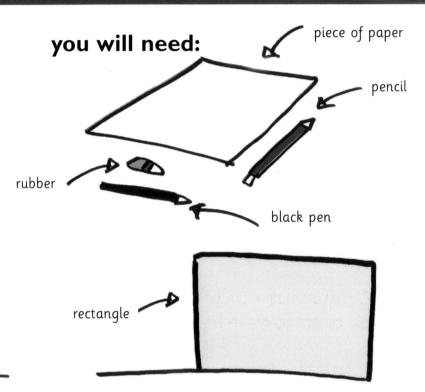

piece of paper

pencil

rubber

black pen

horizontal line

❶ Using a pencil or pen, draw a horizontal line as shown above.

rectangle

❷ Put a rectangle on top of the line as shown to make the body of the truck.

vertical line

❸ Draw two vertical lines – make one the same height as your rectangle and the other half as tall.

step shape

❹ Add three more lines to make a kind of step shape as shown. Now your truck has a cabin.

❺ Along the bottom of your truck, draw a long thin rectangle with three semi-circles cut out of it – one semi-circle should be under the cabin and two under the body.

semi-circles make wheel arches

circle

6 Now draw a circle under each of the wheel arches to make the wheels.

smaller circle

7 Draw a smaller circle inside each of the big circles to make hubcaps.

square

8 Draw a square in the truck's cabin to make a window.

You can colour in your truck however you want. You'll be finished in a flash!

how to draw a BIG truck

Once you have mastered drawing a small truck (see pages 6 & 7), turning this into a bigger truck is easy. You need to stretch the truck's body and make the cabin short and stubby.

you will need:

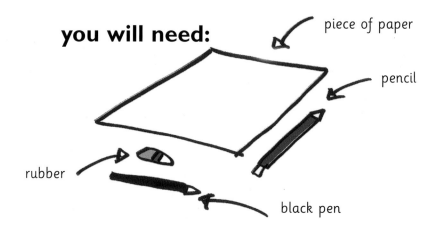

piece of paper

pencil

rubber

black pen

❶ Draw a longer line than the one you started with on page 6 and put a longer rectangle on top of it.

❷ Give the body of your truck some extra wheels then follow the steps below to draw the cabin.

vertical line

curvy line gives stubby shape

triangle

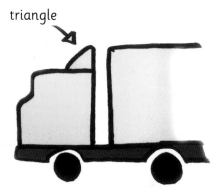

❸ Draw two vertical lines just as I showed you on page 6.

❹ Join the lines as shown to make the cabin shorter.

❺ Draw a triangle on top of the cabin to make a windbreaker.

You could colour in your truck like this.

How about turning your simple truck design into a shiny tanker?

give your truck a sloping bonnet and a window that's more pointed as shown

the body should be cylinder shaped — like a long rectangle with curved ends

put a ladder on the back

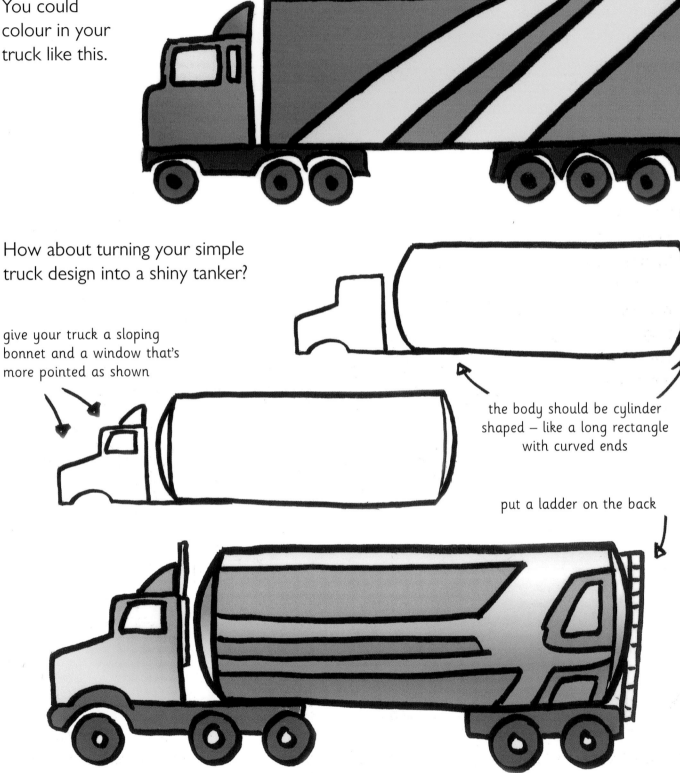

Add the wheels then colour in your tanker so it's ready to speed off the page.

how to draw a truck coming towards you

Now that you know how to draw a truck from the side, it's time to learn how to draw one that's driving straight at you! Remember that the colours I've used here are just to show you which piece to draw – don't colour in your picture until the end.

you will need:

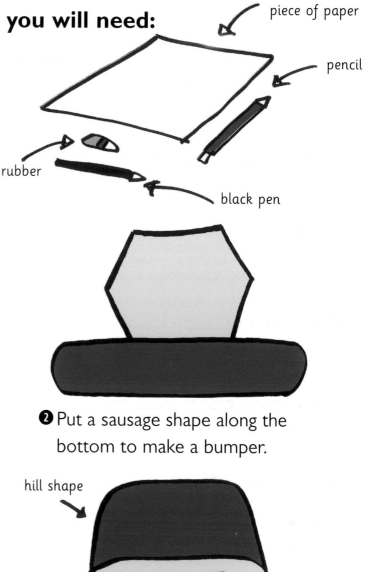

piece of paper

pencil

rubber

black pen

❶ Start by drawing a hexagon as shown – make sure it has six sides.

❷ Put a sausage shape along the bottom to make a bumper.

bonnet

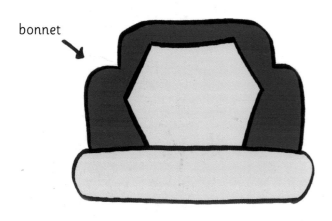

❸ Draw a curvy shape around your hexagon – it will look a bit like an armchair but it's really the bonnet.

hill shape

brick shapes make tyres

❹ On top of the bonnet, draw a kind of flat-topped hill. Then draw two brick shapes under the bumper.

roof

three semi-circles make lights for the top

windscreen

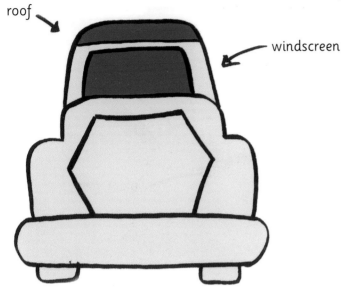

two circles make bumper lights

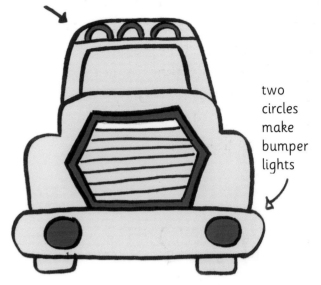

❺ Put a smaller flat-topped hill inside the bigger one to make the windscreen. Draw a horizontal line just above this to make a roof.

❻ Use circles and semi-circles to make lights as shown. Put a smaller hexagon inside the big one and draw lots of lines across it to make an engine grill.

wing mirror

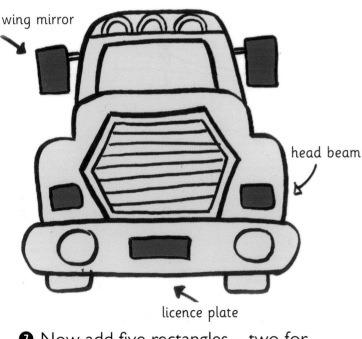

head beam

licence plate

❼ Now add five rectangles – two for wing mirrors, two for head beams and one to make a licence plate.

I've coloured in my truck to make it look like a fire engine. COMING THROUGH!

how to draw a digger

A digger looks like it could grab anything with its pincers – just like a crab.

you will need:

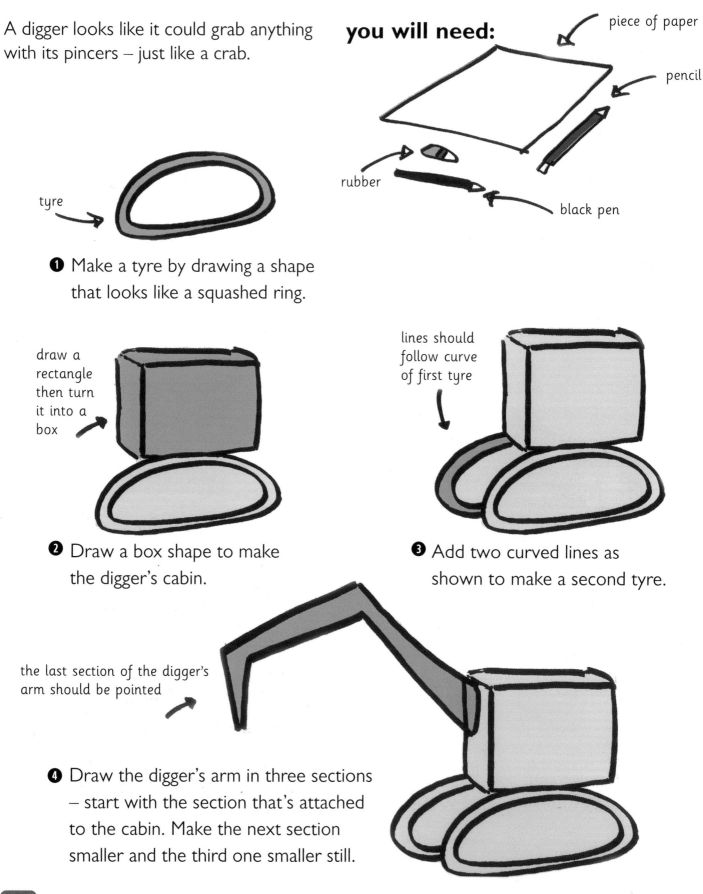

piece of paper

pencil

rubber

black pen

tyre

❶ Make a tyre by drawing a shape that looks like a squashed ring.

draw a rectangle then turn it into a box

❷ Draw a box shape to make the digger's cabin.

lines should follow curve of first tyre

❸ Add two curved lines as shown to make a second tyre.

the last section of the digger's arm should be pointed

❹ Draw the digger's arm in three sections – start with the section that's attached to the cabin. Make the next section smaller and the third one smaller still.

5 Now add the pincers – imagine you are drawing a crab's claw or Captain Hook's hook. Lastly, draw a square on the cabin to make a window.

pincers

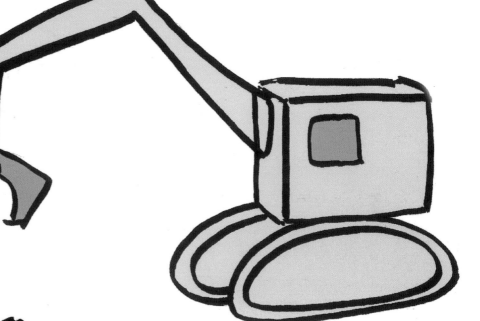

Add a bit of colour and your finished digger is ready for action.

how to draw a terrific tractor

Now let's draw a terrific tractor. In each of the steps below, the part of the picture you need to draw is shaded blue – but don't colour in your own picture until the end.

you will need:

piece of paper

pencil

rubber

black pen

the smallest circle makes the front wheel

straight lines drawn at different angles make the shape of the tractor's body

❶ Draw two different-size circles side by side to make wheels.

❷ Copy the picture on the right to draw the body of your tractor – try drawing a straight line to join the wheels first.

❸ Draw a circle inside each of the wheels. Now you've made some tyres.

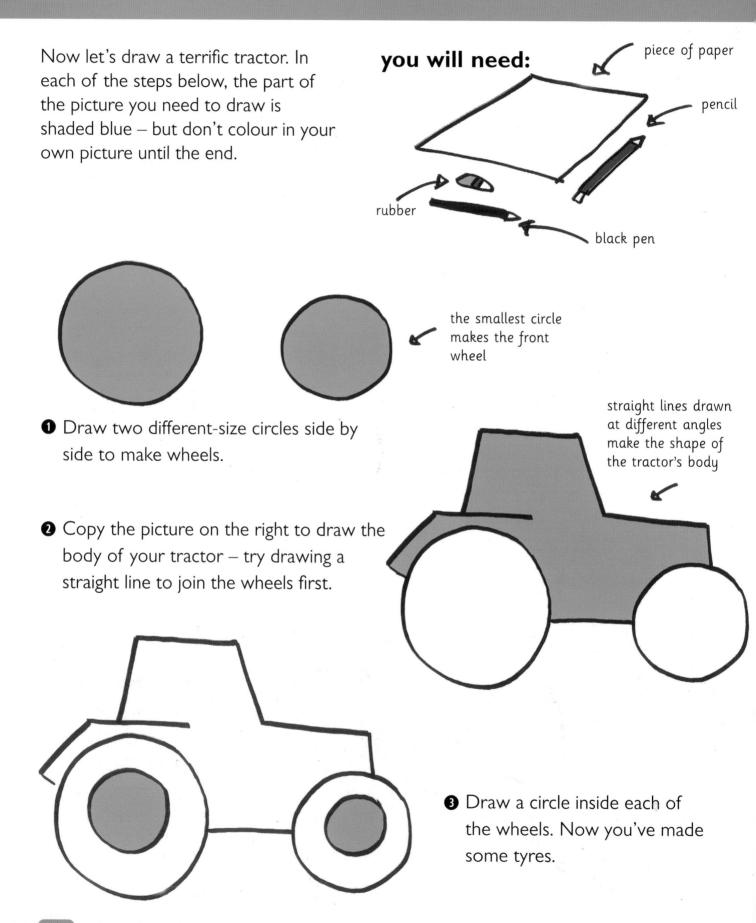

the curved lines look a bit like curls of hair

❹ Draw a much smaller circle in the middle of each wheel. Then draw lots of curved lines around the edge of each tyre to make the tread.

windows

❺ Look at the picture on the right. Carefully copy all the lines I have drawn to make the windows and door. Add stripes to the bonnet too.

❻ You could add a few more details to your picture before you colour it in. Don't forget the cylinder-shaped exhaust pipe – it sticks up out of the bonnet.

how to draw a steam train

Steam trains aren't as hard to draw as you might think. Follow these steps and your train will soon be whistling away.

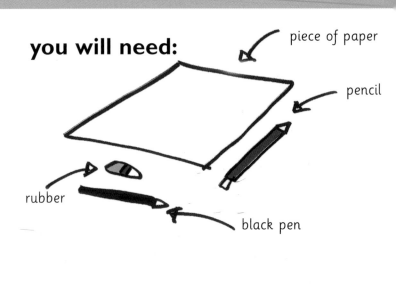

❶ Start with some wheels – draw two identical circles close together.

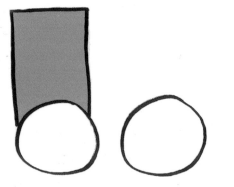

❷ To make the driver's cab, draw three sides of a tall rectangle on top of the wheel on the left as shown.

❸ Draw a long rectangle shape as shown to make the body – leave a curve in it where it meets the other wheel.

❹ Steam trains need to be cleaned inside – so add a curve to make a dome-shaped door and use a tiny rectangle for a handle.

❺ Draw two little circles to the right of your big circles to make front wheels. Now add two arch-shaped windows to the cab.

❻ Draw three rectangles along the top of your train. Put some small circles inside all the wheels then connect the front wheels to the train using little rectangles and lines as shown on the left.

stick shapes

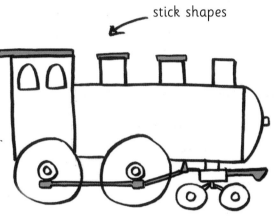

❼ Draw some rods to link the wheels together as shown in the picture on the right. Then draw three thin stick shapes along the top of the train.

steam dome

steam funnel

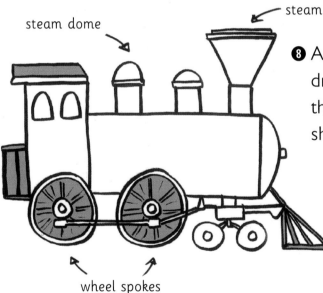

wheel spokes

❽ Add two semi-circles for steam domes and draw a big steam funnel. Study the picture on the left to see what else you could add – I've shaded the extra details green.

❾ Add a bell, some steam and anything else you can think of, then your train will be ready to go running down the track.

how to draw today's trains

Drawing a modern train is a bit like drawing a truck. It's made up of lots of rectangles and circles. Let's start with an ordinary passenger train then look at how we can turn this into lots of different types of train.

you will need:

piece of paper

pencil

rubber

black pen

❶ Draw a long rectangle. Now draw three pairs of circles along the bottom to make wheels.

❷ Put a smaller circle inside each of the circles you've already drawn. Add some little rectangles to make windows and doors.

❸ Your train won't be going anywhere without the driver's carriage. This time, instead of drawing a rectangle, draw a more curvy shape like this one.

curvy nose

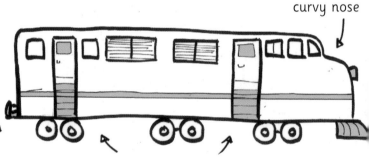

draw a connector so you can add your carriage to the back

you could draw the doors down to the floor

Let's whizz on to drawing high-speed trains.

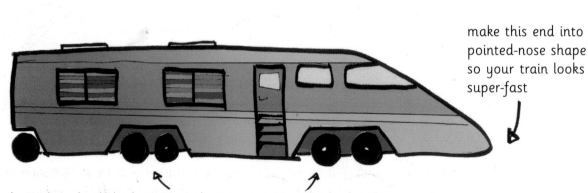

make this end into pointed-nose shape so your train looks super-fast

draw the wheels higher up so they are set into the body of your train

Trains carry all kinds of loads in different types of containers – here are some you could draw.

draw a giant sausage to make a cylinder-shaped tank

pile lots of thin rectangles on top of each other to make planks of timber – the straps holding them on look like long skinny fingers

draw a curvy line above a rectangle to make a heap of gravel – add lots of tiny circles for the little stones

draw patterns on a rectangle like this to turn a carriage into a food container

make a mail truck by drawing an envelope and a stamp on your rectangle instead

to draw a busy train, put some people in the windows – draw stick people if you want. Colour in all your trains before the guard blows the whistle

how to draw some top trucks

Trucks come in all shapes and sizes – here are some of my favourite ones. Once you've mastered using simple shapes to draw them, have a go at sketching them instead. The first one to try is a snowplough.

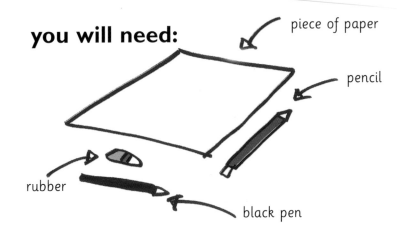

piece of paper

pencil

rubber

black pen

you can draw the back of the truck tipped up as high as you want

shovel

1 First draw three circles to make wheels then join them together with a straight line. Now draw the curvy cab. Put a rectangle behind it, at an angle. Add the shovel.

2 Add a rectangular window and draw four squares to look like panels as shown. Add some more lines to the back of the truck to show how it's being tipped up. Now colour it in.

square panels

3 Now make a rough pencil sketch of your truck. Study the picture on the left – can you see how some parts are made darker by using extra shading? Try it!

build up the shading using layer after layer of soft pencil lines

Now let's draw a cement mixer truck. The trickiest part is the cement mixer itself on the back of the truck – it looks a bit like a diamond, or an ice-cream cone lying down.

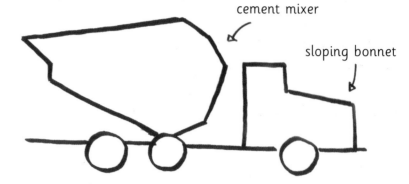

cement mixer

sloping bonnet

❶ As before, start with three circles joined together by a straight line. Draw a cab with a sloping bonnet. Then, starting above the middle wheel, draw an eight-sided shape as shown – the sides are all different lengths.

❷ Use this picture to help you add some more details to your truck then colour it in.

❸ Now try a pencil sketch. As before, draw a rough outline of your truck first. When you are shading, take a break every now and then so you can study your picture to see which parts need more work.

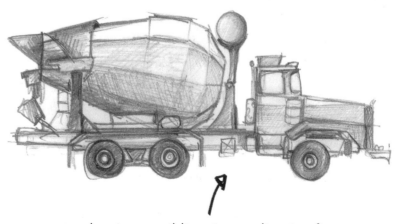

try drawing pencil lines in one direction first then in another direction for the next layer

how to draw two more trucks

On these pages you can find out how to draw a fire engine and a dumper truck. Let's start with the fire engine.

you will need:

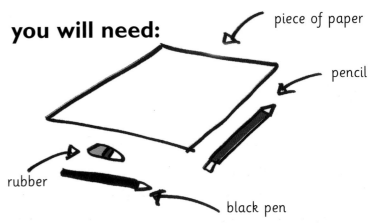

piece of paper

pencil

rubber

black pen

sky lift looks like the letter V lying on its side

boxy-shaped cab

the body should be half as tall as the cab

❶ Draw two circles for wheels. Copy the cab and body you can see in the picture on the left. To make the sky lift, sit a triangle on top of the body then add two diagonal lines. Draw a square dangling from the top.

❷ Add some more details as shown on the right – don't forget the windows. Now colour in your picture – red of course!

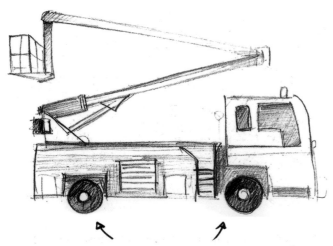

shade some parts more than others to make them darker

❸ Now draw the outline of your fire engine again in pencil. Make the lines very light at first – if you aren't happy with the shape, you can rub out the lines without leaving too many marks. Now add some shading.

A dumper truck has a very distinctive shape.

❶ Start by drawing two wheels and link them together with a horizontal line. Finish off the cab shape as shown on the right. Now add the container – see if you can draw it without taking your pen off the page!

container

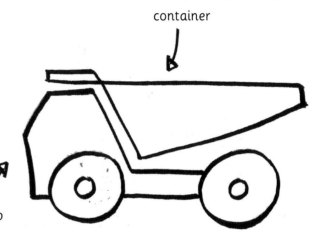

cab

making the rubble is a bit like drawing a cloud

❷ Make some rubble by drawing a line with lots of curves in it. Next draw some windows on your cab. Add a few more details as shown to make your dumper truck even more realistic. Now colour it in.

❸ Next make a pencil sketch. Compare the different parts of the truck with each other to help you get their sizes right. Make sure you are happy with the shape of the truck before you start shading.

the way you shade your picture can show whether a surface is rough or smooth

how to draw a tractor from an angle

So far we've been drawing objects from the side or face on. But what about drawing an object from an angle? Let's take the tractor you learnt to draw from the side on page 14. This time you'll need to show both front wheels, not just one.

you will need:

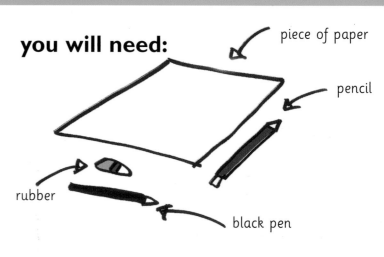

piece of paper

pencil

rubber

black pen

this circle (the back wheel) should be biggest

draw the first front wheel low down

this circle is smaller to make the second front wheel look further away

each curved line makes a crescent-shaped moon

❶ Draw three circles to make wheels. Look carefully at the position and size of each of the circles.

❷ Now draw a curved line in each of your circles to give your wheels their 3D shape.

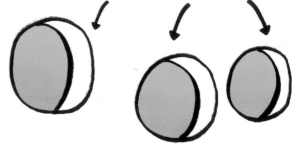

tractor body

now the wheels look like doughnuts!

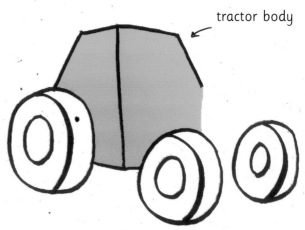

❸ To make the hubcaps, draw a smaller circle inside each wheel.

❹ Next draw the body of the tractor. To start, try drawing a vertical line from top to bottom in between two of the wheels as shown above.

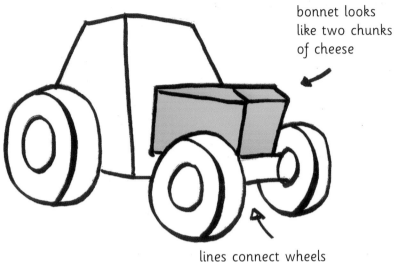

bonnet looks
like two chunks
of cheese

lines connect wheels

❺ Draw two lines to connect the front wheels. Now draw the bonnet above the lines as shown on the left. This is the hardest part so it might take a few attempts to get it right.

❻ The tractor tyres need good tread – you can make this by drawing lots of little sausages! When you've done that, add a circle and a curved line to two of the wheels as shown.

sausage shapes make tyre tread

❼ To finish off, add some windows and a black rectangle for an engine grill. Then colour in your farmyard masterpiece.

25

Collages get you to think about all the different shapes that make up one picture. Make sure you draw each shape in pencil first before you try to cut it out.

This fire engine collage will look best on a piece of black paper.

you will need:

coloured paper

glue

scissors

pencil

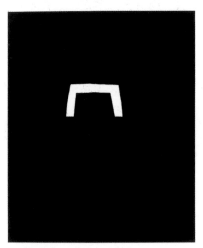

❶ Draw a windscreen shape on white paper. Cut it out and stick it on.

❷ Make the bonnet shape from red paper and stick it on as shown.

❸ Next make a sausage-shaped bumper using some grey paper.

❹ Make the roof from a thin rectangle of red paper – it should be as wide as the windscreen.

❺ Make a hexagon shape from your grey paper and stick it above the bumper to make the engine grill.

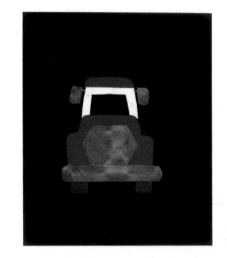

❻ Using grey paper again, cut out two small rectangles for wing mirrors. Use blue paper to make the tyres.

❼ To make lights, draw some small circles on yellow and white paper – try drawing around a coin. Cut them out then cut some of them in half to make semi-circles for the top lights.

❽ Now it's time to start a fire! First draw a big flame shape on a piece of red paper. Cut it out and stick it on your picture. Turn to the next page to find out what to do next.

9 Stick a slightly smaller orange flame on top of your red flame. Put a smaller yellow flame on top and finish by adding an even smaller white flame.

10 Now make some more multi-coloured flames. The picture below reminds you how to build up the colours — make sure you cut out a smaller shape each time.

red   orange   yellow   white   =   multi-coloured flame

11 Now draw a big zig-zag shape on a piece of red paper. Carefully cut out the middle part but don't throw either part away.

12 Stick the red zig-zag frame you've made over your picture as shown.

13 Lay your red zig-zag shape on a sheet of blue paper and draw a bigger zig-zag shape around it. Cut out the middle part so you are left with a blue zig-zag frame.

14 Stick the blue zig-zag frame over the red zig-zag frame.

15 Lastly, draw 12 stick shapes on a piece of yellow paper and cut them out. Stick them around the two head beams to make the lights dazzle. Brilliant – is that the siren I can hear?

how to draw a monster truck using colouring pencils

Now that you've mastered drawing in pencil, try using some colouring pencils.

you will need:

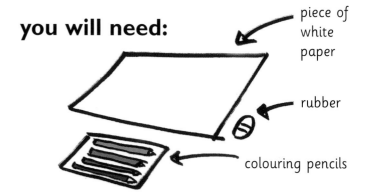

piece of white paper

rubber

colouring pencils

❶ Using a dark blue or black colouring pencil, lightly draw the outline of an action scene. Try copying this monster truck – it's driving off a ramp into a ring of flames.

❷ Start shading the monster truck by drawing layer after layer of little lines. Draw the lines for each new layer in the opposite direction to the ones you drew before. This is called cross-hatching. Use yellow and orange for the circle of fire.

❸ Go around the flame using a bright red. Add some fire to the back of the truck.

❹ Now shade the wheels with a black. Use it to make the edges of the wheels thick and curly

❺ Now colour in the ground – I've used green, blue, brown and a little black.

❻ Use a blue colouring pencil for the fence and black for the ramp.

❼ Fill in the crowd by drawing lots of rough circles – put a smiley face on some of them. Colour in the rest of the picture as shown then use your colours to go over the whole of the picture again to give it more texture. Let's go!

how to make a moving truck using pastels

You can create some great effects with chalk pastels. Like colouring pencils, pastels are easy to draw with but you can also blend and layer the colours a bit like you can when you use paints.

you will need:

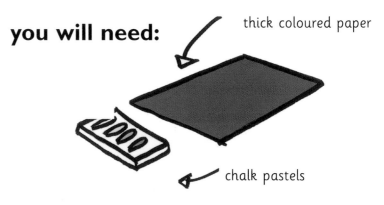

thick coloured paper

chalk pastels

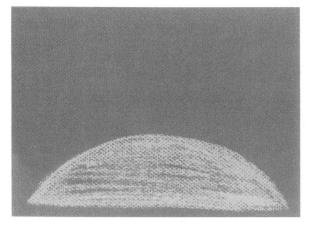

❶ Take a bright green pastel and draw a large semi-circle to make a hill shape. Now shade it in.

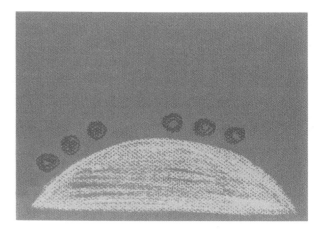

❷ Using a strong blue pastel, draw six little circles above the hill shape as shown. These are your truck's wheels.

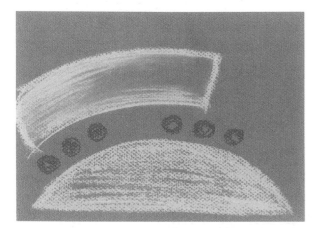

❸ Now take a lighter blue to give your truck a curved body as shown. Smudge the colour at the back of the truck with your thumb.

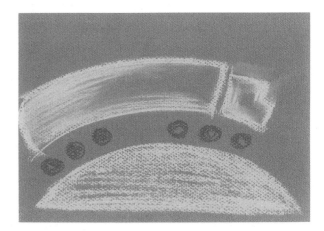

❹ Use the same blue to draw the cab. Look back at the first few pages of this book if you need to practise drawing the cab. Then smudge the colour as before.

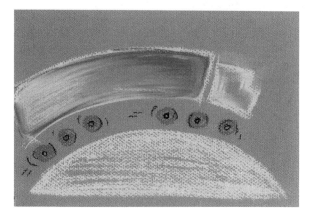

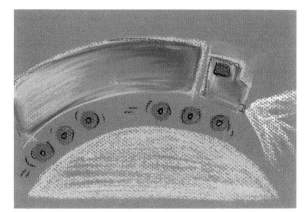

5 Take a black pastel and draw a small circle inside each wheel. Add some little curves around the wheels so they look like they are moving. Outline the truck's body in purple then smudge in the colour at the front using your thumb.

6 Do the same with the truck's cab. Now use a darker blue pastel for the cab window. To make the headlight beams, draw some rough lines in front of your truck using a white pastel. Then add a few more lines using a yellow, as shown.

7 Now go over the outline of the truck again with black and add a bit more shading as shown. What do you think?

how to paint a train travelling through the mountains

You can make this colourful scene using just four paints – blue, red, yellow and white. Mix these paints together to make all the other colours.

you will need:

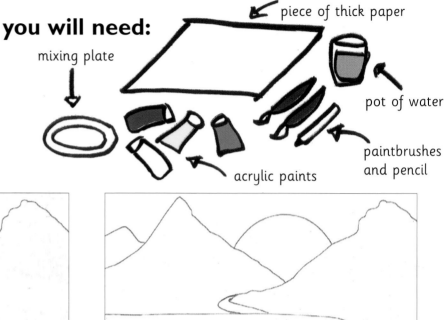

mixing plate

piece of thick paper

pot of water

paintbrushes and pencil

acrylic paints

❶ First, draw your picture in pencil. Don't forget the train.

❷ Mix blue and yellow paints together to paint the grass green.

❸ Add a bit more blue to the green to make a darker shade. Use it to start painting the mountain on the right, working from the bottom up. As you get nearer the top, add some white to the paint to make it lighter.

❹ Now paint the mountain to the left of the sun. It should be paler than the mountain on the right as this will make it look further away. Make the mountain behind it even paler. Then mix some yellow with a tiny amount of red to paint the sun.

❺ Next get ready to paint the sky. Add a lot of red to some yellow paint, then add a little bit of white – this will make the sky look misty. What a spectacular sunset!

❻ Mix some blue paint with a little bit of white to paint the river. Start at the bottom of your picture and add more white to the paint as you go along. Next mix blue, yellow and red to paint the bridge brown.

❼ Carefully paint a blue stripe on the train then wait for this to dry. Now add some white to your blue paint. Using your smallest paintbrush, paint some little rectangles and lines on the train to make windows and doors. Zoom!

how to paint a fun tractor scene

For my next picture, you can use poster paints or inks. This painting gives you the chance to play around with drawing lots of different patterns and shapes.

you will need:

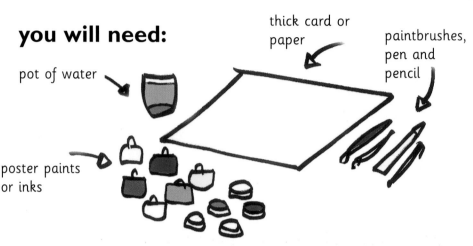

thick card or paper

paintbrushes, pen and pencil

pot of water

poster paints or inks

❶ Draw all of the picture in pencil first. It's really important that you do this before you start painting. Then colour in your tractor one section at a time.

❷ Now use a yellow to paint the field where your tractor is working – leave the circles white.

❸ Next paint the curly blades at the back of the tractor so they're ready to spin round and dig up the ground.

❹ Now paint the field on the left of your tractor as shown. Start with a purple and use it to paint every other row.

❺ Now use a blue to paint the rows that you missed out last time.

❻ Paint the strips of grass and the leafy trees green. Make the tree trunks brown.

❼ Now paint the other strips of ground orange.

❽ Paint the field at the back a strong pink. Use dark red for the stars.

❾ Next paint the sky orange. Let the picture dry, then use a black felt-tip pen or a ballpoint pen to draw round every shape, including the fence posts. See how bold it looks now?

how to paint a colliding truck

I think you'll really enjoy these pages. They show you how to turn a moving truck into a collision scene. You can do this all on one piece of paper.

you will need:

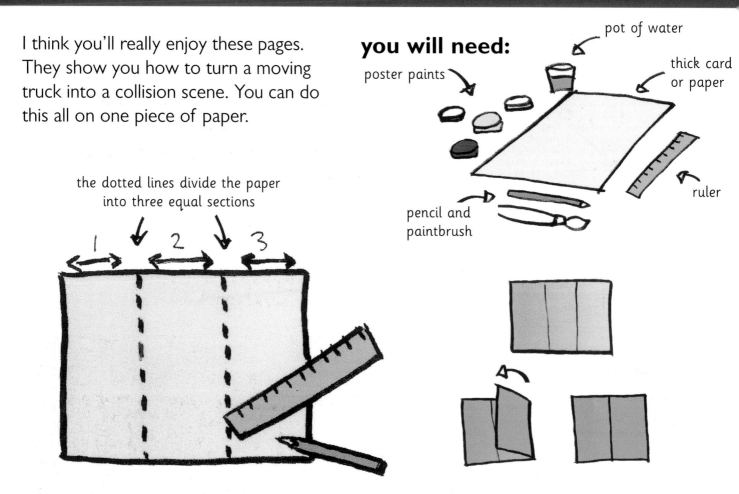

pot of water

poster paints

thick card or paper

pencil and paintbrush

ruler

the dotted lines divide the paper into three equal sections

1   2   3

❶ Measure the long side of your piece of paper then divide this by three – ask an adult to help you with this if you need to. Draw two dotted lines in pencil to mark the three equal sections. Later you will be folding the paper as shown above right.

❷ With your piece of paper opened out, make a pencil drawing of the crash scene you can see on the page opposite this one. Draw your truck on a sloping line so it looks like it is speeding downhill. Make sure the truck stretches across more than half of your piece of paper. Draw one of the car wheels up in the air and add some dramatic zig-zag shapes too.

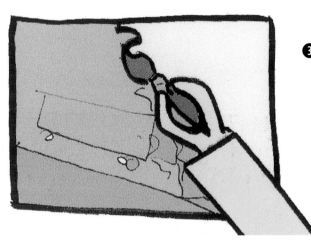

❸ Next use your poster paints to make your picture as bold and bright as possible. You could copy the colours in the picture below.

❹ Your finished picture should look a bit like this. Use a dark blue or black for the background to make it seem as if it's the middle of the night.

❺ Wait for your painting to dry then fold the right-hand third of the page inwards. This should cover up the damaged part of your truck, as well as the car. Now turn to the next page of this book to find out how to fix your truck!

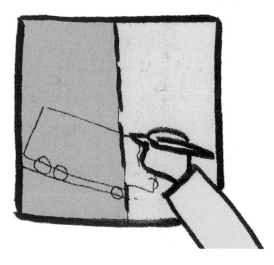

6 On the white part of your folded piece of paper, draw the front section of your truck again. This time the truck should be driving along the road in perfect condition! The picture below should help you to draw it. Make sure your truck's new front section lines up with the back part of the truck that you drew before.

7 Now you're ready to paint your new drawing. Use exactly the same colours as you used before so that the two sides of your new scene match to make one perfect picture.

8 To show movement, draw some white lines in the sky above the front of your truck and around the front wheels as shown.

❾ Wait for the paint to dry then see how your picture of a high-tech truck unfolds...

❿ ...to reveal a WRECK!

how to use watercolours to paint a scrapyard

Even a scrapyard can look lovely when it's painted in watercolours. You need to paint your picture on thick paper that hasn't been coated as your colours must be able to soak into the paper.

watercolour paper or thick cartridge paper

watercolours

pot of water

pencil, rubber and paintbrushes

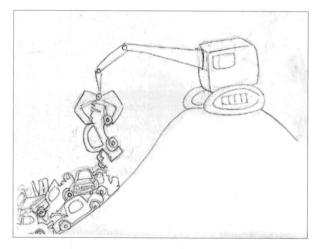

❶ Draw your picture in pencil first. If there are any parts you're not happy with, rub them out and draw them again.

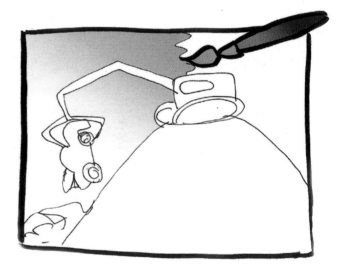

❷ Next dip a clean paintbrush in your pot of water and brush over the sky with water only. Then dip the paintbrush into your blue paint – don't overload your brush. Now paint over the sky again.

❸ Scrunch up a tissue to make a ball then use it to dab some areas of the sky. This technique is really effective for making clouds – but make sure the paint is still wet when you do this or it won't work!

❹ Paint the hill with a green. Then using a clean brush, paint the machine strong pink.

❺ Next paint the wheels brown. Use lots of different colours to paint the cars.

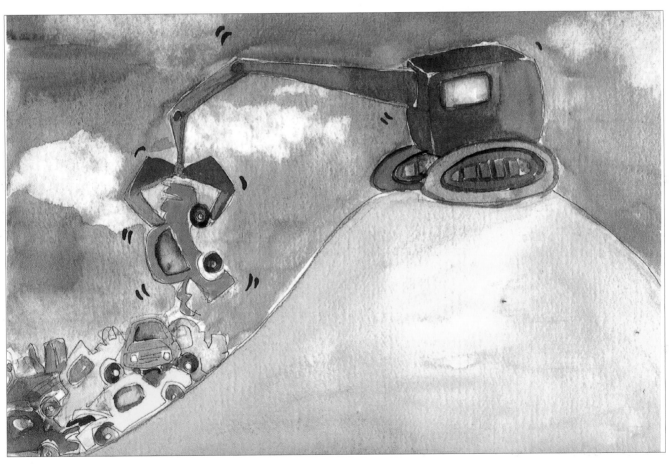

❻ You should always use your darkest colour last – so now outline different parts of your picture in black as shown. Put some little curved lines around the arm of your machine and around the car that its pincers are gripping, to show movement. Great!

how to draw a super steam train in pastels

Earlier in this book (on pages 32 & 33), I showed you how to draw a simple picture of a moving truck using pastels. Here you can learn how to use pastels to create a much more detailed picture – this time let's draw a moving steam train.

you will need:

pastels

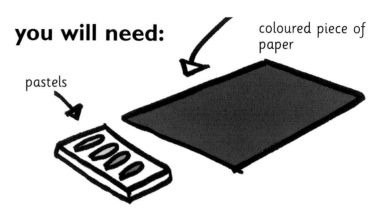

coloured piece of paper

❶ Use a brown chalk pastel to draw a rough outline of your travelling train as shown.

❷ Pick a green chalk pastel and, using the side of the chalk instead of the end, shade in the grass.

❸ Shade parts of the sky blue then fill in the gaps with white chalk to make clouds. Use your thumb to blend the two colours together where they meet.

❹ Draw some lights on the front of the train using a yellow pastel. Use the yellow to draw some windows on the carriages too.

❺ Outline the front section of your train again using a darker brown or black. Use your thumb to smudge the chalk into the parts of the train you have outlined.

❻ Do the same for the rest of the train. Add some black to the sky to make steam.

❼ Now wash and dry your hands to get rid of the black. Take a purple chalk pastel and use it to outline the train again then smudge the colour into the body of the train as you did before. Add some white here and there, as shown.

❽ Now outline the windows with a black chalk pastel as shown, then use the black to go over a few other parts of your picture – like the big headlight. Time to get going.

how to use lots of art materials in one steam train scene

For each of the colourful pictures in this book, we've used either colouring pencils, chalk pastels, acrylic paints, watercolours, poster paints or inks. But what about using some of these different colouring materials together in one picture? Let's experiment.

you will need:

watercolours

pot of water

thick card or paper

white wax crayon and pencil

colouring pencils and paintbrush

❶ Take a piece of thick card or watercolour paper and make a rough pencil drawing of your scene. Don't forget the sheep – their bodies are like fluffy little clouds.

❷ Use a white wax crayon to go over the parts of the picture that you want to stay white. I've used my crayon for the steam billowing out of the train's funnel and for the sheep's fleeces.

❸ Use a green watercolour to paint the field in front of your train. Don't worry about going around all the sheep as the paint will glide over their waxy backs.

❹ Use brown watercolour paint for the brick wall around the tunnel – you can brush right over the steam and once again, the wax will stay white.

❺ Now use a lighter green watercolour to paint the back field. Remember that using a paler shade, makes things look further away.

❻ Choose a red watercolour to paint your steam train. Now turn to the next page of this book to find out how to finish off your great work of art.

❼ Add a dab of blue to the white paint on your saucer. Mix them to create a bluey white. With a fresh cotton bud paint some long wispy clouds over the sun and sky.

❽ This part is very simple. Use some yellow paint to create a polka dot effect over the back hill.

❾ Finally, using either some black paint, a marker pen or even a biro, draw in the sheep's stick legs and oval heads. Painting with cotton buds is a very simple technique, yet it creates a very effective painting.